# MY WILD LIFE
# I am a bear!

By Camilla de la Bedouere

Miles Kelly

Look out for the 'Ask for help!' boxes. You will need help from an adult to do these activities.

Ask for help!

First published in 2012 by Miles Kelly Publishing Ltd
Harding's Barn, Bardfield End Green, Thaxted, Essex, CM6 3PX, UK
Copyright © Miles Kelly Publishing Ltd 2012

10 9 8 7 6 5 4 3 2 1

**Publishing Director** Belinda Gallagher
**Creative Director** Jo Cowan
**Editorial Director** Rosie McGuire
**Editor** Sarah Parkin
**Designers** Jo Cowan, Joe Jones
**Image Manager** Liberty Newton
**Production Manager** Elizabeth Collins
**Reprographics** Stephan Davis, Anthony Cambray, Jennifer Hunt

ISBN 978-1-84810-619-2

Printed in China

British Library Cataloguing-in-Publication Data
A catalogue record for this book is available from the British Library

## ACKNOWLEDGEMENTS

The publishers would like to thank Mike Foster (Maltings Partnership), Joe Jones, and Richard Watson (Bright Agency) for the illustrations they contributed to this book.

All other artwork from the Miles Kelly Artwork Bank.

The publishers would like to thank the following sources for the use of their photographs:
t = top, b = bottom, l = left, r = right, c = centre,
bg = background, rt = repeated throughout

### BOOK
**Cover** (front) Hung Chung Chih/Shutterstock; (back, tr) Geoffrey Kuchera/Shutterstock, (bl) Petrmasek/Dreamstime
**Alamy** 18 Arco Images GmbH
**Dreamstime** 5(giant panda) Hungchungchih, (sloth bear) Mvshiv, (moon bear) Karelgallas, (American black bear) Hilbell; 7(t) Petrmasek
**FLPA** 10 Jules Cox; 12 Theo Allofs/Minden Pictures; 13(t) Jules Cox; 14 Katherine Feng/Minden Pictures; 15(b) Jules Cox; 19(t) Matthias Breiter/Minden Pictures, (b) Terry Whittaker
**Fotolia** 8–9(bg) bluesky; 16–17(bg) Kirsty Pargeter
**Nature Picture Library** 15(t) Axel Gomille
**Photo Discs/Digital Stock** 5(brown bear)
**Photo Discs/ImageState** Heading panel(rt)
**Shutterstock** Joke panel(rt) Tropinina Olga; Learn a Word panel(rt) donatas1205; 1 Jim Chagares; 2 Envita; 3 Eric Isselée; 4–5 Ilya Akinshin; 5(sun bear) Cuson, (spectacled bear) Matt Hart; 6 Richard Seeley; 7(b) Khoroshunova Olga; 8(brush stroke tl) Ambient Ideas; 9(paint splatter tl) sabri deniz kizil, (l) Anna Ts, (br) jennipenni89; 11(b) Antoine Beyeler; 13(r) Marcin Niemiec; 16(paper tl) sharpner, (berries tl) Andra Popovici, (panda panel tr) jennipenni89, (b) donatas1205, (bear b) VectorZilla; 17(paper cl) House @ Brasil Art Studio, (bl) MisterElements; 20–21 Dennis Donohue; 21(r) Uryadnikov Sergey

### POSTER
(clockwise from tl) Pete Oxford/Minden Pictures/FLPA, Jules Cox/FLPA, Paul Sawer/FLPA, Eric Isselée/Shutterstock, Vladimir Wrangel/Shutterstock, Patrick Endres/Visuals Unlimited/Corbis

### STICKERS
All images are from Shutterstock. (teddy head tl) Paul Winward, (panda cub tc) molchunya, (polar bear br) andere, (bear in den bc) Shaber, (black bear bl) MisterElements

Every effort has been made to acknowledge the source and copyright holder of each picture. Miles Kelly Publishing apologizes for any unintentional errors or omissions.

Made with paper from a sustainable forest

www.mileskelly.net
info@mileskelly.net
**www.factsforprojects.com**

# Contents

# What are you?

## I am a bear!

I am a kind of animal called a mammal. Mammals have warm blood, fur or hair, and we feed our babies on milk.

Powerful shoulders

Big snout

Small eyes

Q. How do you make a bear run fast?

A. Shout, "Ready, teddy, go!"

Four strong legs

Thick,
furry coat

Polar bear

there are eight types
of bear and most of
them live in forests.

 Brown bear

Giant panda

Sloth bear

Sun bear

Spectacled bear

Moon bear

 American black bear

Large paws

# What do you eat?

## I eat fish!

I am a type of brown bear called a grizzly. I stand by the river's edge and catch the fish that swim past me.

Bears mostly eat berries, roots, leaves and fruits.

## Yummy ants

Sun bears have very long tongues. They use them to lick up grubs, ants and honey.

## Hungry bear

Giant pandas eat bamboo, which is a type of tall grass that grows in China. Pandas need big, strong teeth to chew the bamboo.

Q. What is a polar bear's favourite fast food?

A. Ice burgers!

# Activity time
## Get ready to make and do!

Ask for help!

## Teddy bear picnic

Invite your friends and their teddies to a teddy bear picnic. Ask an adult to help you make a healthy one.

## Draw me!

YOU WILL NEED: pencils · paper

1. Draw a squashed circle. Add two rounded shapes for ears.

2. Now draw the body, small tail and two legs.

3. Add the eyes, nose and mouth, and draw two more legs.

Now colour me in and give me a name!

8

# Paper bag bears

Ask for help!

## YOU WILL NEED:
brown paper bag
brown paper
scissors · glue
pens · pencils

## HERE'S HOW:
1. Fold the bottom corners of the bag to make a face shape.
2. Cut out two ears and two paws from the paper. Stick them on the bag.
3. Draw the bear's face.

If you have a white paper bag and black paper, try making a panda puppet.

# Bear flapjacks

## YOU WILL NEED:
125 g butter · 100 g brown sugar
5 tbsp golden syrup
250 g rolled oats · 20 g raisins
20 g chopped nuts

## HERE'S HOW:
1. Turn on oven to 180°C (Gas 4).
2. Gently heat the butter, sugar and syrup in a saucepan.
3. Stir in the oats, raisins and nuts.
4. Pour the mixture into a 20 cm square baking tin and squash it down a bit with a spoon.
5. Bake for 30 minutes. Then cut into squares and allow to cool before taking out of the tin.

Ask for help!

# Where do you live?

## I live in the forest.

There are mountains and rivers nearby.
I live here because there is lots of
food for my cubs.

## Sleepy time

Females look after their cubs in dens, which are safe holes under trees or rocks. Bears rest in dens when it is cold outside.

## Cold life

Polar bears live in the icy north. Their thick white coats keep them warm. They have huge paws that help them run across the slippery ice.

**Q.** Why do polar bears wear thick coats?

**A.** Because they'd look silly wearing woolly hats!

# How fast can you run?

## I can run very fast.

Even though I am a large, heavy animal, I can charge at 50 kilometres an hour!

Q. Have you ever hunted bear?
A. No, but I have been hunting with my clothes on!

Running

**Swimming**

# In the water
Polar bears love to swim.
They can hold their breath
underwater for two minutes.

# In the trees
Bears are good at
climbing. They use
their sharp claws to
help them grip trees.

**Climbing**

### LEARN A WORD:
**charge**
When one animal runs
at another animal to
attack it.

13

My babies
are called cubs.

My cubs are just 15 centimetres long when they are born. I carry them gently in my mouth.

Giant panda

## Piggyback

Sloth bear mums carry their cubs on their backs until they are about nine months old.

## Growing up

Bear cubs love to play and pretend to fight. When they are old enough, they leave their mothers to find new homes of their own.

Q. What do you call a grizzly bear that's been caught in the rain?

A. A drizzly bear!

# Puzzle time

## Can you solve all the puzzles?

### Berry feast

Bryan the bear has five berries. One of his friends has three berries, and another friend has two. How many berries do the three bears have altogether?

### True or false?

1. All bears have fur.
2. Polar bears live in warm forests.
3. A baby bear is called a kitten.

### Tell us apart

There are three differences between Barney and Billy – can you spot them?

**Barney**          **Billy**

GROW!

## Rhyme time

Only four of these words rhyme with 'bear'. Can you find them?

chair  ear  cub  pear
spear  fair  deer
furry  hare  den

## Who caught the fish?

Use your finger to trace each fishing line and discover which lucky bear caught the fish.

**Belinda**

**Bethany**

**Bertha**

Find the answers on page 25.

# What do you look like?

## I have light fur around my eyes.

These eye markings make it look like I am wearing glasses!

Spectacled bear

## Ghost bears

Some American black bears are born with white coats, which make them look like ghosts.

## Moon marking

Moon bears have a large white mark on their chests, which looks like a crescent moon.

**Q.** What goes black, white, black, white, bump?

**A.** A panda rolling down a hill!

# Are you scary?

## All bears can be dangerous.

We have powerful muscles and are very strong. We also have large jaws, big teeth and sharp claws.

Q. Why wasn't the bear hungry?

A. Because he was stuffed.

# People and bears

Most bears are shy animals and they are easily frightened. They prefer to stay away from people.

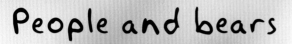

## Deadly bears

Adult male polar bears will have fights. They stand tall and growl at each other.

**LEARN A WORD:**

**claw**

An animal's large, sharp nails are called claws.

# Goldilocks and the Three Bears

*Use your stickers to illustrate the story.*

**Once upon a time,** there was a little girl called Goldilocks. Her mother had told her never to go off on her own, but one day, Goldilocks sneaked down a path that led into the forest. Soon she was lost. At last she saw a light through the trees. It  was coming from a cottage. She opened the door and went in.

On the table inside were three bowls of porridge. The big bowl was too tall for her to reach. The middle-sized bowl was too hot. But the little one was just right, so she ate it all up.

By the fire were three chairs. Goldilocks couldn't climb up

onto the big chair. The middle-sized chair was too hard. The little chair was just the right size for her, but as soon as she sat down, it broke into pieces.

Goldilocks went upstairs and found three beds. The big bed was too hard. The middle-sized one was too soft. But the little one was just right, and soon she was fast asleep.

Then the three bears who lived in the cottage came back. Father Bear growled, "Who has been eating my porridge?" Mother Bear grumbled, "Who has been eating my porridge?" Baby Bear gasped, "Who has been eating my porridge, AND has eaten it all up?"

The bears saw the chairs. Father Bear  growled, "Who has been sitting in my chair?" Mother Bear grumbled, "Who has  been sitting in my chair?" Baby Bear gasped, "Who has been sitting in my chair, AND has broken it?"

The bears went upstairs. Father Bear growled, "Who has been sleeping in my bed?" Mother Bear grumbled, "Who has been sleeping in my bed?" Baby Bear gasped, "Who has been sleeping in my bed, AND is still there?"

Just then, Goldilocks woke up. She ran from the bears and out of the door. She found her way home and promised never to wander off again.

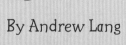

By Andrew Lang